# AFTER THE BLACKOUT

POEMS

J. R. ROGUE

# CONTENTS

# AFTER THE BLACKOUT

Goodreads Choice Nominated poet J.R. Rogue's newest poetry collection—After The Blackout—explores the author's experiment to give up alcohol for a year. And how it transformed into a new way of life.

Weaving between debilitating hangxiety and the gross marriage between alcohol and her sexual encounters, the author tears down memories and walls to expose the black and white definition of alcohol abuse society feeds us. And brings the stark truth to the surface—the face of alcohol use disorder can be anyone, and any reason to give up alcohol is valid.

This collection is about everything we lose and the ways we let ourselves go.

And in the end—how to reclaim peace.

# SIGNS OF AN ALCOHOL USE DISORDER (AUD)

To be diagnosed with alcoholism, individuals must meet any two of the below criteria within the same 12-month period:

• Using alcohol in higher amounts or for a longer time than originally intended.

• Cravings, or a strong desire to use alcohol.

• Continuing to abuse alcohol despite the presence of a psychological or physical problem that is probably due to alcohol use.

• Being unable to cut down on alcohol use despite a desire to do so.

• Spending a lot of time obtaining, using, and recovering from the effects of alcohol.

• Continuing to abuse alcohol despite negative interpersonal or social problems that are likely due to alcohol use.

• Giving up previously enjoyed social, occupational, or recreational activities because of alcohol use.

• Being unable to fulfill major obligations at home, work, or school because of alcohol use.

• Using alcohol in physically dangerous situations (such as driving or operating machinery).

• Having a tolerance (i.e. needing to drink increasingly large or more frequent amounts of alcohol to achieve desired effect).

• Developing symptoms of withdrawal when efforts are made to stop using alcohol.

Free National Helplines

• SAMHSA: **1-800-662-4357**

• National Suicide Prevention: **1-800-273-8255**

• National Youth Crisis: **1-800-442-4673**

• Boys Town: **1-800-448-3000**

• Drugfree.org: **1-855-378-4373**

# PRAISE FOR AFTER THE BLACKOUT

Reading this collection of poetry just pulls you in. It's a
powerful way to move forward.
**— DANIELE, GOODREADS REVIEW**

If I had to give it as many stars as tears I shed, it would be
thousands. This is all of us. Insanely relatable and emotionally
raw. My favorite to date.
**— LINDSEY DOMOKUR, GOODREADS REVIEW**

Wow…I commend Rogue's honesty and her ability to bare
herself on the page. This collection was stunning, it hurt at
times but in the most beautiful way…if you've struggled with
alcohol, if you haven't, if you know someone who has, it's an eye
opening look at what society deems a *normal addiction*.
**— SHANNON O'CONNOR, AUTHOR**

These words are like a mirror for the darkest days of my life.
Such a beautiful disaster.
**— S. ZAPATA, AUTHOR**

★★★★★
This was a book of knives and I felt every single one of them.
— **CHÈRI-LEE FISHER, GOODREADS REVIEW**

★★★★★
Her poetry is a dark truth, but there is also a sense of relief as
we reach the recovery stage.
— **DARLENE RODRIGUEZ, AUTHOR**

For everyone who has supported me
+ loved me as I recovered.

CONTENT WARNING:

suicidal thoughts, alcohol consumption, & non-consen-
sual sex

# NOTE FROM THE AUTHOR

On January 1st, 2020, I embarked on an experiment to give up alcohol for a year. Though my drinking habits had changed significantly from my hard partying years, I was still concerned about how I used alcohol. In 2019, I brought a bottle of Fireball to my table for a book signing to calm my nerves & be less socially awkward—to make everyone else more comfortable. This has been a theme in my life since the first time I got drunk, at 18 years old. I drink to make others more comfortable. I drink to make social situations more manageable. I never believed I had a drinking problem because of the way I used alcohol—I was a social drinker, I never drank home alone, with a bottle of wine, & therefore convinced myself everything was okay. I told myself lies. Unfortunately, we are sold a black & white definition of alcoholism & alcohol abuse. Alcoholics are those who get kicked out of bars, those who lose their jobs, the homeless man on the corner. These extremes—& society's romanticism of alcohol consumption—cause many to never seek help.

I believe it is vital to show others that the face of alcohol abuse can be anyone, & any reason to give up alcohol is valid. You don't have to hit a black & white image of rock bottom to quit. My rock bottom was the way I felt during hangovers. I thought I was alone, & no one else had suicidal thoughts in the days proceeding drinking. But in my early sober days, I read a lot—something I do before embarking on any life change—& discovered I wasn't alone in hangxiety. I'll leave a list of reading recommendations at the end of this book.

Finally, I want to touch on alcohol abuse & its marriage to my sexual encounters, as the bulk of this book will explore that toxic relationship. I wrote this collection through the lens of a white cis woman engaging in heterosexual sex. Therefore, I do not aim to speak for anyone but myself & my own experiences.

On October 26, 2001, I lost my virginity. On October 27, 2001, I got drunk for the first time. My relationship with sex has always been grossly intertwined with my relationship with alcohol. Beyond my first sexual encounter, I cannot recall engaging in an initial sexual encounter with a new partner without alcohol present. Most sexual abuse survivors are looking to reclaim a sense of control in their lives. I avoided sex & alcohol in high school because the thought of letting myself go to either felt like giving up control. Unfortunately, over time, I convinced myself that I could regain a sense of control when I had drunk sex with men during my manic singles days because I could *have sex like a man*, or be the *cool girl* society sells us. I thought if I could control the way men felt about me, I would regain power, but what I ultimately achieved was losing control of my memories, who I was, & my self-worth.

This collection is about everything I lost, the ways I let myself go, & in the end—the way I reclaimed peace. & how an experiment became a new way to live.

# I CAN'T LOOK AT MY OLD POETRY ANYMORE

I can't look at that girl—

that wounded bird

spilling herself all over,

vodka veins

& sloppy confessions

convincing herself that the

warm glow of bar lighting

brought her closer to men who

only wanted to get under her clothes.

# THE SLOW DECAY OF SELF

it is a slow death—the rushed

& smudged giving away

of flesh to hungry mouths

& wanting hands that

seek not to remember middle

names & your favorite color.


it is a slow death—

unpeeling of flesh,

smudged lipstick, & panting keens.

the sweat & the sunlight glinting

reminders of the want for the grave

when the drugs wear off—

blue-collar remorse,

white skin,

milky tears adorned.

it is a slow death—a welcome reprieve

from the voices mingling

& muttering the truth inside,

the slow decay of self.

*enough* is a word slipping away.

# WHAT A STRANGE THING TO DESIRE

what a high to chase—

that warm dream.

that perfect slow descent

into showing everyone

in the room exactly who I am not,

but who they want me to be.


what a ~~tonic~~ toxin to race for,

what a slow spiral into

madness to achieve.


what a strange thing to desire.

# COOL GIRL

I am not the

cool girl anymore.

I am not the easy laugh,

the blackout prey.

I am not the trauma hidden,

the supplicant lay.

I am not mid-day wine laugh.

I am not the girl

who fucks you simply

because you want it.

I am not the easy girl,

the cool crisp vodka.


I am not what you want me to be.

# YOU ARE NOT EIGHTEEN ANYMORE

you loved him, & you waited.

eighteen & *new new new*.

you lost yourself in the front

seat of his mom's

car on a cliffside.

& the next night,

you lost yourself by the

open mouth of an Ozark cave.

Downhome Punch & a punch to the

reality you knew.

the cops spit gravel

when they found you,

& the lies fell from his

mouth like honey.

you didn't know

what would come later—

the parties,

the shattered glass on the wall

as you screamed in his face.

Jack Daniels & Johnny Walker red nights.

a jackknife to the heart

& the two were

wed & bed you.

liquor & the way

he licked the salt from your neck.

it's been 18 months since you had a drop,

& you are not eighteen anymore.

your fingers are tired,

but you can unravel the

noose tying *loose woman* & *daddy issues*

around your red red neck like

a dog tag for a war you never signed up for.

LURE ON THE TRAPS

his name was ~~Isaac~~,

but the experience

was not religious.


you cried the next day at work

thinking of the way he touched you—

the way you let yourself blackout,

& let go.


*the cool girl*

*the ladies' night*

*lighting rod.*


he texted again, & you set the trap.

*who is this?*

*no, this isn't her number.*

free drinks,

& you were the price,

the snare,

the lure on the traps,


but it only cut you.

# HEADBOARDS CRACKING

his name was ~~David~~,

& he would have begged for a biblical life.

easy smile, broad chest.


you said he wasn't your type,

& then there he was at the bar,

& he was *so patient*.

he was the *nice guy*.

& you don't remember a thing.


you think he lasted

for just a moment

because *god,* he had *wanted this*.

you think you cried when he said he

wanted to take care of you.

*he was lost too*, but maybe

he remembers

the way your soft body felt.

maybe he remembers

the sound of walls crumbling

& headboards cracking.


maybe he could hear your

regret the following day

when he said he wanted

you to meet his family.


maybe he thinks

you're still a nice girl

even though you never

spoke to him again.

# I ROMANTICIZED IT

we don't talk about

the fact that the bouncer wouldn't

let me in because I was too drunk.

we don't talk about

the tears I spilled on the wrought iron

table outside & the way my heart

was slashed & bruised.

we don't talk about

the water he fed me,

& the shoes I broke.

we don't talk about

the fact that I left my phone

behind & left who I was on the street

corner as I faded into the

dark with a stranger.

we don't talk about

the fact that I couldn't drink

a drop the next day.

we don't talk about

how I romanticized it in poetry—

the way I tried to make it okay.

we don't talk about

the double vodka.

we don't talk about

the way I can't fuck in daylight.

we don't talk about

the way we undress to the

bone for men looking for a warm home.

we talk about how I fucked a country

singer that night.

*what happens in Nashville stays in Nashville.*

we talk it into normalcy.

we push our cries into the grave.

# WEAPON

these useless memories are

the only useful

weapon I have left to wield

against the lies I tell myself—

*maybe one drink will be okay?*

# SPIRITS

I hold you here—
in these pages
where heartache can live.
where the promise
of happily-ever-after
doesn't haunt the keyboard.


you're not a man, not a promise.


you're the thief—
the mirage that glimmered
when the drinks fell fast.


& now, as my eyes see the sun,
I do not find you.

I find only the remnants

of another

love ~~laced~~ tainted with spirits.

# AS THE FOG ROLLS IN

it's warm—

the slow roll of my

defenses coming down.

it sounds romantic—

walls crumbling,

loose lips & loose limbs,

the electric feel of his hand on my leg,

the way his mouth touches

my neck in a dimly lit elevator.


it's warm—

the way he unravels my intentions,

my thoughts,

the arch of my back,

& the quick of my breath.

it's warm—

the shame & the thoughts

of ending my own life the next morning.


as the fog rolls out,

the shattered glass comes into focus.

the blood on my hands

& the blood on his bed.


we are all close to animals then,

when the drink is amber,

& the smoke lingers till morning.


as the fog rolls in,

I forget the day,

forget the way the

mundane calms & the walls

of my haven are comfort.


as the fog rolls in,

I step into the night

& taste the salt of my prey—

turn up my belly,


pretend I am the electric

feel of their salvation.

pretend the decay

doesn't taste like malt,


like I have been here before,

& all I want to do is break away.

# GASPING, GROVELING

it's a midnight thing.

not always midnight,

but somewhere between

waking & passing out—

not sleep, but that heavy crash

of *never again, & what a thrill.*

the gasp in the open window,

the plea for *no more*

slow fading into the abyss.


I repeated the dance,

the beige top, the strappy sandals.

the quiet remembrance

of the way they touched me.


the way I begged

for their inhabitance.

the way I prayed

for a way to forget my name.

to ignore

the way the daylight hours crowed.

the way the waking waltz

was becoming mundane.


I am grasping for crisp air—

groveling at the feet

of those who harm,

pressing needy fingers into supple flesh.


I am the nightmare,

the constant loop.

I am the midnight model

of all my bad intentions—

the plea,

the please,

the pleasure I can

only feel when numbed

& laughing over jokes that hold no humor.


what a thrill to dangle so close to death.

what a thrill to fuck the past away.

it's a midnight thing.

the slow decay of every

clear-eyed move forward.


it's a wading into the abyss,

the one I crawled back to again & again.

# CONSENT

where did *no* go?

it sunk in her belly,

churning & writhing.

shipwrecked with

consent she never intended to give.

her head was as heavy as his body.

laughter danced upon the

midnight lawn below

their window.

screams that die in swollen

throats cannot dance with the air.

he spread her legs

& pushed inside, once, twice, ~~gone~~.

he didn't finish, so they say *no harm, no foul.*

she never said *no,*

so they say she probably *wanted it.*


she reaches for lost moments.

she convinces herself

that maybe the devils are right.

# WHERE GIRLS GO TO DIE

I know places

where girls go to die.


the apartment in Nashville.

the hotel room in Vegas.

the room on 6th street.

the back of that SUV

where no one remembers the name of the bar.

the hood of that old Hyundai.

the trailer by the bonfire.

the mattress in the basement with no sheet.


I know places where girls go to die.

don't ask me how I know.

don't ask me because

I can't remember how I got there.

someone lost

hold of my hand.

some whiskey breathed

devil kissed my smile away.


the front seat, the bluff before us.

the tiny studio.

the houseboat that rocked with us.


I know places where girls go to die.

I tried.

# PLAY DEAD

*I like you better when you're drunk.*


spread me open,

see the parts within.

red wires & jolts of light.

parted lips & words

that refuse to be sensible.

a mumbled *thank you,*

a half-hearted rejection.


*god, you're fun.*


pull out the daddy issues, the kink,

the shadows—

trauma & tantalizing lies.

open me up & find the dead zones,

the ancient offerings wrapped in silk.

*you laugh more.*

this is me, & I am half right—
quiet peace with an open gullet.
pour in the poison,
see how I can dance for you in back alleys
& the bedrooms of men
I don't even like.

*I love your smile when you've had a few.*

tell me all the ways I can
make you *more comfortable,*
how I can be *nice,*
how I can laugh at your shitty joke
& make you feel at peace.

open me up
& tell me where the amber goes.
the regret & the way your
smile fades when the
porcelain calls for my overindulgence.

*the sex is great like this, you're so free.*

tell me you can keep me safe.


open me up & tell
this beating heart it is
not enough for a casual dinner.
tell it to lie down, play dead.


open me up, tell me what you like.
tell me what you want to drown.

# SORROW SIDE UP

my gums are bleeding again.

that stubborn molar makes me ache.

& every Wednesday,

like clock work, I tried to die.

only to be regretfully resurrected

every third Thursday.

# BOTH FEET OFF THE GROUND

he kissed you there,

behind the ear,

lifted you off the ground,

carried you to the bed

you would stumble from

the following day,

wondering where you'd

been & why him—

*what a smile,*

*what do one-night-stands*

*do for poetry?*

you stared in the mirror

eyeliner smudged,

extensions falling out,

red lipstick like a brand.

coming down isn't easy.

coming to terms with the map

& the destination is vital.


he kissed you there,

in the hollow of your throat,

where your words died

& the *kind* you slithered out—

*what's a one-night-stand*

*when you can barely stand yourself?*


what a smile, what a slow slide.

your face is on the floor,

& you can't keep

dropping everything.


he lifted you off the ground,

& your legs went around,

& you don't believe in god or regrets

or the virtues of men,


but you believe you won't

hate your face one day.

won't despise this black heart,

this ~~arrogance~~ mania,

this stare in the mirror.

coming down isn't easy—

walks of shame do

dangerous things to poetry.

# NOT TODAY

it was simple to start it that way.


want to go out for a drink tonight?
*not today. I'm busy. I'm reading a good book.*
*I have to work out. my husband is needy, can't leave.*


not today, turns into a week, maybe more.
& they love you less.


you are no longer the confidant.
the laughing two of hearts.
you are no longer the wing woman.
you are no longer the good time—
the blackout memories.
the *everyone loves her when she gets like this.*
you are no longer

*the less scary version of yourself.*

you are no longer the knife.

you are the lake,

& they are afraid to wade into you.

*not today* turns into a year, turns into more,

& who are you to them now?

a ghost.

the fragment of their

blackout imagination.

their lost memories.

you are not longer the beat,

the passenger singing to the night air.

you are no longer the manic mess they knew,

but you are healthy & alive,

& every feeling is breaking you open,

flaying the inside.

it was simple to start it that way.

*do you want to numb yourself?*

you ask the mirror,

& she smiles, something kind.

*not today.*

*let's feel it all today.*

# NICK

in the nick of time, he changed your mind about high school bullies & first dates with small-town legends. in the nick of time, you found the dark bedroom to sleep the dizzy off. in the nick of time, he found you warm & blackout. in the nick of time, he undressed you. he pushed your pushing hands away. in the nick of time, he pushed in, just a little. in the nick of time, you pushed him away again, & he passed out—blacked out into oblivion, & you slept beside his bloated face. in the nick of time you snuck out the next morning, & never spoke to him again.

# IN FOUR, OUT SIX

you can't imagine it not

being like this—in four, out six


the breath an old friend,

life & pressure,

slow control,

but you gasped for it—in four, out six.


an obsession of the heart,

countdown till the streets go dark,

& the maniacs took hold of the night.


life is a decay.

the slow unraveling

of self-taught walls—

brown amber, in four, out six into the bowl.

you cried for it,

strangers holding your hair,

& a twisted ankle.


they want you like that again—

amiable,

the laughing face,

& the loud laugh.


you can't imagine not being

like this—the slow shut of a door,


the windows open,

& the peace rolling

down the hallway.

this is home.

this is the slow unraveling

of a life that

does not need

to be lived in snapshots—

frantic texts,

the morning-after regrets.


the breath comes easy now—in four, out six

an old friend, long left dead.

control, revived.

# A COCKTAIL OF THE GOOD & THE BAD

it's hard to explain,

so I find myself only spending

time with those who

do not ask me for an explanation.


& those who dare ask,

I give them the basics;

no need to scare anyone away

unless they ask for it.


*oh, I hated being hungover / I'm just trying to be healthier / I guess I'm is just getting old.*


*no, I didn't have a drinking problem / not the way you think / I can't control myself / no, I didn't drink often—but when I did / I couldn't control myself / I couldn't control what I said.*

drunk mouths do no speak sober thoughts.

what a laugh, what prison to live in for years.


*oh, I hated being hungover / no, I don't miss it / sometimes, when I was hungover / I wanted to kill myself / no, the shame couldn't break away / in the end / every time / I wanted to kill myself.*


it's pretty hard to explain until you

& let the ugly slither up their arm.

it was a cocktail of the good & the bad.


what a smiling time, what a laugh.

what a way to wake up,

wanting to never wake up.


when the bad makes you want to die,

what gold is the good?

# I GET TO REMEMBER

there is space for you—
when the room is dark.
I turn on my side,

the blankets rustle
like leaves in autumn,

I bend my knees
& glance
over my thighs.

you break in like
waves, with your tender
hands. the cat runs away,
jumps off the bed.

& I get to remember

everything we do.

# GENTLE OFFERING

how do I tell you,

from his safe space,

that it's not normal

to feel the way I felt?


rip my skin open,

flee the room,

drown the humming in clear liquid

that could give life to an automobile.


to shoot my tender pieces with malt,

with poison-laced confessionals.


how do I tell you,

from this safe space,

all the ways I never want to go back?

I offered myself

a year & in return was given clear eyes,

the gentle offering

of who I really am.


& no morning shaded

with the rushing waves

of death by hands meant to

bring me closer to salvation.

# RECOVERY

& those who love you?

they will not wield

your fears & faults.

they will not forge weapons

from your weakness, your worries

to slip slowly into your back.

they will hear *recovery* & say

*I cannot wait to see who you're bringing back to me.*

J. R. Rogue first put pen to paper at fifteen after developing an unrequited high school crush and has never stopped writing about heartache. She has published multiple volumes of poetry and novels. Her work has been recognized with three Goodreads Choice Awards nominations, a testament to the impact of her work on readers.

Rogue lives in the Midwest with her family, enjoying a peaceful life reading and telling stories.

**RIGHTS**

If you would like to learn more about foreign language and audio adaptations, please contact Two Daisy Media.

**GET IN TOUCH**

You can contact J.R. Rogue through her website or by connecting with her Substack.

You can also join her mailing list to keep up with everything she's working on.

www.jrrogue.com
www.jrrogue.substack.com
contact@jrrogue.com

# ALSO BY J. R. ROGUE

Romance

### *MUSE & MUSIC SERIES*

Breaking Mercy

Burning Muses

Background Music

Blind Melody

### *SOMETHING LIKE LOVE SERIES*

I Like You, I Love Her

I Love You, I Need Him

I Like You, I Hate Her

Romantic Suspense

### *RED NOTE SERIES*

The Rebound

The Regret

The Return

Supernatural Suspense

### *OZARK OMENS SERIES*

The Girl Next Door

### *STANDALONE NOVELS*

Kiss Me Like You Mean It